BREAKING BARRIERS
EMPOWERING WOMEN
IN THE WORKPLACE

REMI KUTI

In a world where gender equality remains an ongoing struggle, I am excited to announce my forthcoming book, "Empowering Women In The Workplace: Unlocking the Potential of Women in the Workplace." This book highlights the importance of empowering women and creating a more inclusive and diverse work environment. By delving into the challenges, sharing inspiring stories, and offering actionable strategies, I hope to ignite a conversation and drive meaningful change.

The Power of Empowering Women Exploring the Significance of gender equality in the Workplace and its Impact on Individuals, organisations, and Society and Debunking Myths and Misconceptions about Women's Capabilities and Highlighting the unique strengths they bring to the table.

Breaking Barriers and Overcoming Bias Examining the barriers and biases that hinder women's progress in the workplace, including stereotypes, unconscious bias, and gender-based discrimination. Providing insights and practical tools to challenge and overcome these obstacles. Creating Inclusive Work Cultures, Highlights the importance of fostering inclusive work environments where all voices are heard, respected, and valued. Offering strategies to build diverse teams, promote inclusivity, and cultivate an atmosphere of mutual support and collaboration.

Developing Leadership Skills Discussing the development of essential leadership skills among women, including effective communication, assertiveness, negotiation, and resilience. Sharing inspiring stories of successful women leaders and extracting valuable lessons from their journeys.

Nurturing Career Growth and Advancement Guiding advancing women's careers, including mentorship, sponsorship, networking, and strategic career planning and addressing the unique challenges women face in navigating career progression and offering practical advice for overcoming them.

Balancing Work and Life Recognizing the importance of work-life balance and discussing strategies for managing competing priorities, overcoming guilt, and fostering well-being. Exploring the evolving dynamics of caregiving responsibilities and advocating for supportive policies and flexible work arrangements. Conclusion: In "Empowered: Unlocking the Potential of Women in the Workplace," I invite readers to join the movement toward gender equality. By empowering women, we not only enhance individual lives but also strengthen organizations and society as a whole. Let's embrace diversity, challenge biases, and create a future where women are given equal opportunities to thrive and contribute their unique talents. Together, we can build a more inclusive and equitable world.

Note: Feel free to customize the chapter titles and content to align with your specific focus and approach.

Table of Contents

Introduction

Definition of Empowering Women

Empowering women is a term that has gained significant attention in recent years. It is a concept that is essential to achieving gender equality and creating a more just and fair society.

Empowering women symbolizes providing them with the necessary skills, knowledge, and resources to take control of their lives and make informed decisions about their future. It involves breaking down social, cultural, and economic barriers that prevent women from reaching their full potential.

Empowering women in the workplace means creating an environment where women have equal opportunities to succeed and advance in their careers. It involves ensuring that women are paid the same as their male counterparts, that they have access to the same training and development opportunities, and that they are supported in their efforts to balance work and family life.

Empowering women in sports means providing them the same opportunities as men to participate in sports and compete at the highest levels. It involves breaking down gender stereotypes and ensuring that women are portrayed in all aspects of sports, from coaching and manager politics.

Empowering women in politics means providing them with the resources and support they need to participate fully in the political process. It involves ensuring that women have equal representation in government and that their voices are heard on issues that affect their lives.

Empowering women in education means providing them with the skills and knowledge they need to succeed in their careers and in life. It involves ensuring that girls have access to the same educational opportunities as boys and that they are encouraged to pursue careers in traditionally male-dominated fields.

Empowering women in entrepreneurship means providing them with the support and resources they need to start and grow successful businesses. It involves breaking down barriers that prevent women from accessing funding and other resources and ensuring that they have the same opportunities as men to succeed in business.

Empowering women in leadership means providing them with the skills and training they need to lead effectively and make a positive impact in their communities. It involves ensuring that women have equal representation in leadership positions and that they are supported in their efforts to make a difference.

Empowering women in technology means ensuring that they have the same opportunities as men to participate in the growing field of technology. It involves breaking down stereotypes that prevent women from pursuing careers in technology and providing them with the skills and training they need to succeed.

Empowering women in finance means ensuring that they have equal access to financial resources and that they are not discriminated against in lending and investment decisions. It involves breaking down barriers that prevent women from achieving financial independence and providing them with the skills and knowledge they need to manage their finances effectively.

Empowering women in the arts means ensuring that they have equal opportunities to express their creativity and pursue their passions. It involves breaking down stereotypes that prevent women from pursuing careers in the arts and providing them with the support and resources they need to succeed.

Empowering women in health and wellness means ensuring that they have access to the same quality healthcare as men and that their specific health needs are addressed. It involves breaking down barriers that prevent women from accessing healthcare and providing them with the resources and support they need to maintain good health and wellness.

Overall, empowering women means creating a world where women have equal opportunities to succeed and achieve their full potential. It requires a concerted effort from individuals, organisations, and governments to break down barriers and ensure that women have access to the resources and support they need to thrive.

The Importance of Empowering Women

In today's world, empowering women is more important than ever before. Women have made significant progress over the years, but they continue to face challenges in various areas of life such as the workplace, sports, politics, education, entrepreneurship, leadership, technology, finance, the arts, and health and wellness. Empowering women is essential for the advancement of society as a whole and for achieving gender equality.

Empowering women in the workplace is crucial for creating a diverse and inclusive work environment. When women are given equal opportunities, they bring unique perspectives and ideas to the table, which can lead to increased innovation and productivity. Women who feel empowered are also politics in their jobs, leading to a reduction in turnover rates and increased employee satisfaction.

In sports, empowering women is essential for promoting gender equality and creating role models for young girls. When women are given equal opportunities to participate in sports, they can develop their skills and compete at the highest level. This can also lead to increased support and recognition for women's sports, which can help to break down gender stereotypes and promote equality.

Empowering women in politics is vital for creating a more representative and inclusive government. When women are given equal opportunities to participate in politics, they can bring a unique perspective to policymaking and help to create policies that benefit all members of society. Women who hold political office can also serve as role models for young girls, inspiring them to pursue careers in politics.

In education, empowering women is crucial for ensuring that girls have equal access to education and can achieve their full potential. When women are educated, they are more likely to participate in the workforce, leading to increased economic growth. Empowering women in education also helps to break down gender stereotypes and promotes gender equality.

In entrepreneurship, empowering women is essential for promoting economic growth and reducing poverty. When women are given equal opportunities to start and grow businesses, they can create jobs and contribute to the economy. Empowering women in entrepreneurship also helps to break down gender stereotypes and promotes gender equality.

Empowering women in leadership is crucial for promoting diversity and inclusion in all areas of life. When women are given equal opportunities to lead, they can bring unique perspectives and ideas to the table. Empowering women in leadership also helps to break down gender stereotypes and promotes gender equality.

In technology, empowering women is essential for creating a more diverse and inclusive tech industry. When women are given equal opportunities to participate in technology, they can bring unique perspectives and ideas to the table, leading to increased innovation and productivity. Empowering women in technology also helps to break down gender stereotypes and promotes gender equality.

Empowering women in finance is crucial for promoting economic growth and reducing poverty. When women are given equal access to financial services, they can start and grow businesses, invest in education, and participate in the workforce. Empowering women in finance also helps to break down gender stereotypes and promotes gender equality.

Empowering women in the arts is vital for promoting diversity and inclusion in the arts industry. When women are given equal opportunities to participate in the arts, they can bring unique perspectives and ideas to the table, leading to increased creativity and innovation. Empowering women in the arts also helps to break down gender stereotypes and promotes gender equality.

Empowering women in health and wellness is essential for promoting gender equality and improving health outcomes for women. When women are empowered to make decisions about their own health and wellness, they can take control of their lives and improve their overall well- being. Empowering women in health and wellness also helps to break down gender stereotypes and promotes gender equality.

In conclusion, empowering women is essential for promoting gender equality and creating a more diverse and inclusive society. When women are given equal opportunities to participate in various areas of life, they can bring unique perspectives and ideas to the table, leading to increased innovation and productivity. Empowering women also helps to break down gender stereotypes and promotes gender equality, creating a better world for everyone.

Why Breaking Barriers is Important

Breaking barriers is important because it opens up opportunities for everyone. When we break down barriers, we create a level playing field where everyone has an equal chance to succeed. This is important for women in particular because women have been historically excluded from many fields and industries.

Empowering women means giving them the tools and resources they need to succeed. This can mean providing mentorship programs, networking opportunities, and access to funding and business resources. It also means creating policies and practices that support women in the workplace, such as flexible work arrangements, paid parental leave, and equal pay for equal work.

When women are empowered, they can make a significant impact in their communities and in the world. Women in politics, for example, can bring a unique perspective to policy-making and can advocate for issues that affect women and families. Women in education can serve as role models and mentors for young girls, encouraging them to pursue their dreams and reach their full potential. Women in entrepreneurship can create businesses that address social and environmental issues and promote sustainable development.

Women in leadership can inspire others to follow their lead and create positive change in their organizations. Women in technology can bring fresh perspectives and ideas to the tech industry, which has traditionally been male-dominated. Women in finance can promote responsible and sustainable investing practices that benefit both people and the planet. Women in the arts can use their creativity to challenge stereotypes and promote diversity and inclusion. Women in health and wellness can advocate for policies that promote access to healthcare and support for mental health and wellbeing.

Breaking barriers is not just important for women, but for society as a whole. When we empower women, we create a more equitable and just world where everyone has the opportunity to thrive. It is up to all of us, men and women, to work together to break down barriers and create a better future for all.

Empowering Women in the Workplace

Challenges faced by Women in the Workplace

Despite significant progress in gender equality, women in the workplace still face several challenges that hinder their advancement and limit their potential. These challenges are common across various sectors, including sports, politics, education, entrepreneurship, leadership, technology, finance, arts, and health and wellness. Some of the significant challenges faced by women in the workplace are discussed below.

Gender bias and stereotypes

One of the primary challenges faced by women in the workplace is gender bias and stereotypes. Women are often stereotyped as being emotional and less capable of handling leadership roles. This bias often leads to women being overlooked for promotions or leadership positions, even when they are qualified. Additionally, women are often paid less than men for the same job, which further perpetuates gender inequality.

Work-life balance

Women often struggle to balance their work and personal lives due to societal expectations and responsibilities. Women are expected to take care of the home and family, which often conflicts with their work schedules. Additionally, women who choose to have children often face discrimination in the workplace, with some employers assuming that they will not be committed to their jobs.

Lack of representation

Women are often underrepresented in leadership positions, which limits their potential and hinders their advancement. Women need role models and mentors to help them navigate the workplace, and a lack of representation can make it difficult for them to find support and guidance.

Sexual harassment and discrimination

Sexual harassment and discrimination are significant challenges faced by women in the workplace. Women are often subjected to unwanted advances, comments, or behaviour and that make them uncomfortable and can result in a hostile work environment. Additionally, women may face discrimination based on their gender, race, or sexual orientation.

In conclusion, women in the workplace face several challenges that hinder their advancement and limit their potential. These challenges are familiar across various sectors, and addressing them requires a concerted effort by both men and women. By working together to eliminate gender bias and stereotypes, promoting work-life balance, increasing representation, and eliminating sexual harassment and discrimination, we can create a more equitable and empowering workplace for women.

Overcoming Gender Stereotypes

Gender stereotypes have been a major hindrance to women's empowerment, especially in the workplace. Stereotypes are beliefs or assumptions about the characteristics, abilities, and roles of individuals based on their gender. These stereotypes limit women's potential, restrict their choices, and create barriers to their success. However, it is possible to overcome gender stereotypes and empower women to reach their full potential.

The first step in overcoming gender stereotypes is to recognize and challenge them. Many people hold unconscious biases that reinforce gender stereotypes. Men and women should examine their own beliefs and attitudes about gender and work to overcome any biases they may have.

This can be done by seeking out diverse perspectives, challenging assumptions, and being open to new ideas.

Another important step in overcoming gender stereotypes is to provide women with the same opportunities, resources, and support as men. This means ensuring that women have equal access to education, training, and development programs. It also means promoting women into leadership positions, creating inclusive workplace cultures, and providing flexible work arrangements that accommodate the needs of both men and women.

Empowering women in sports, politics, education, entrepreneurship, leadership, technology, finance, the arts, and health and wellness needs a multi-faceted approach. It requires a commitment from both men and women to challenge gender stereotypes and create a more inclusive and equitable society. It also requires a recognition that empowering women benefits everyone, not just women.

In sports, for example, empowering women means providing equal opportunities and resources for women athletes, coaches, and officials. It means challenging the notion that women's sports are inferior to men's sports and promoting gender equality in all aspects of sports.

In politics, empowering women means promoting women's representation and leadership in government. It means challenging the gender stereotypes that suggest women are not fit for leadership roles and providing women with the support and resources they need to succeed in politics.

In education, empowering women means promoting girls' education and providing equal opportunities for women in all fields of study. It means challenging the gender stereotypes that suggest women are not as capable as men in certain subjects and ensuring that women have the same access to education and training as men.

In entrepreneurship, empowering women means providing women with the resources, funding, and support they need to start and grow successful businesses. It means challenging the gender stereotypes that suggest women are not as innovative or entrepreneurial as men and creating a more supportive and inclusive business environment for women.

In leadership, empowering women means promoting women into leadership positions and providing them with the support and resources they need to succeed. It means challenging the gender stereotypes that suggest women are not as effective leaders as men and creating a more inclusive and equitable workplace culture.

In technology, empowering women means promoting women into technology careers and providing them with the training and development they need to succeed. It means challenging the gender stereotypes that suggest women are not as skilled or interested in technology as men and creating a more inclusive and diverse technology industry.

In finance, empowering women means promoting women into finance careers and providing them with the support and resources they need to succeed. It means challenging the gender stereotypes that suggest women are not as capable or interested in finance as men and creating a more inclusive and equitable finance industry.

In the arts, empowering women means promoting women artists and providing them with the support and resources they need to succeed. It means challenging the gender stereotypes that suggest women are not as creative or talented as men and creating a more inclusive and diverse arts community.

In health and wellness, empowering women means providing women with the resources and support they need to achieve optimal health and wellbeing. It means challenging the gender stereotypes that suggest women are not as inquisitive in or knowledgeable about health and wellness as men and creating a more inclusive and accessible healthcare system for women.

In conclusion, overcoming gender stereotypes is crucial to empowering women in all aspects of life. It requires a commitment from both men and women to challenge stereotypes, promote gender equality, and create a more inclusive and equitable society. By working together and supporting each other, we can break down barriers and empower women to reach their full potential.

Bridging the Gender Pay Gap

The gender pay gap is a persistent issue that has plagued workplaces for decades. Despite the progress made in the fight for gender equality, women still earn less than men in most industries and occupations. This gap is particularly pronounced for women of color and those in lower-paying jobs.

The causes of the gender pay gap are complex and multifaceted. Discrimination, unconscious bias, lack of representation in leadership positions, and occupational segregation are all contributing factors. However, there are steps that both individuals and organizations can take to bridge the gap and ensure that women are paid fairly for their work.

One important step is education. Women need to be aware of their rights and the laws that protect them from pay discrimination. Organizations can provide training and resources to help employees understand the importance of pay equity and how to negotiate for fair compensation.

Another key step is transparency. Organizations should be transparent about their pay practices and make sure that their compensation systems are fair and equitable. This includes conducting regular pay audits and addressing any disparities that are uncovered.

Representation is also crucial. Women need to be represented in leadership positions and given equal opportunities for advancement and promotion. This not only helps to close the pay gap but also creates a more diverse and inclusive workplace.

Finally, government policies can play a role in bridging the gender pay gap. Legislation such as the Equal Pay Act and the Lilly Ledbetter Fair Pay Act have helped to protect women from pay discrimination, but more needs to be done. Processes such as paid family leave and affordable childcare can also help to address the systemic barriers that women face in the workplace.

Bridging the gender pay gap is not just a women's issue – it is a social problem that affects everyone. By working together, we can create a more equitable and just workplace for all.

Women in Leadership Positions

Women have come a long way in breaking barriers and achieving leadership positions. Despite significant progress, there is still a long way to go before women achieve parity with men in top leadership positions. This is unusually true in industries such as technology, finance, and politics, where women remain underrepresented.

Empowering women in leadership positions is crucial for creating a more equitable workplace and society. Women bring unique perspectives and skills to the table that can benefit organisations and communities. Research shows that companies with diverse leadership teams perform better financially and are more innovative and adaptable.

There are several ways to empower women in leadership positions. First, we need to challenge gender stereotypes and biases that limit women's potential. Leaders can create inclusive cultures that value diversity and support women's career advancement. We also need to provide women with the resources and opportunities they need to succeed, such as mentorship, training, and networking opportunities.

In sports, women are breaking barriers and achieving leadership positions as coaches, athletic directors, and executives. However, women still face significant challenges in this male- dominated industry, such as unequal pay and lack of representation in leadership positions. Empowering women in sports requires addressing these systemic issues and providing women with equal opportunities to succeed.

In politics, women are making significant strides, with more women than ever before serving in Congress and running for political office. However, women still face significant barriers, such as sexism, misogyny, and gender bias. Empowering women in politics requires addressing these barriers and supporting women's political ambitions.

In education, women are breaking barriers and achieving leadership positions as school administrators and college presidents. However, women still face challenges such as gender bias and unequal pay. Empowering women in education requires addressing these issues and supporting women's Leadership aspirations.

In entrepreneurship, women are making significant strides, with more women than ever before starting and running their own businesses. However, women still face challenges such as access to funding, networks, and resources. Empowering women in entrepreneurship requires addressing these challenges and providing women with the tools and support they need to succeed.

In technology, women are breaking barriers and achieving leadership positions as engineers, developers, and executives. However, women still face significant barriers, such as gender bias and unequal pay. Empowering women in technology require addressing these barriers and providing women with equal opportunities to succeed.

In finance, women are making significant strides, with more women than ever before serving in leadership positions in banking, investing, and accounting. However, women still face challenges such as gender bias and unequal pay. Empowering women in finance requires addressing these challenges and providing women with equal opportunities to succeed.

In the arts, women are breaking barriers and achieving leadership positions as directors, curators, and producers. However, women still face challenges such as gender bias and unequal pay. Empowering women in the arts requires addressing these challenges and providing women with equal opportunities to succeed.

In health and wellness, women are breaking barriers and achieving leadership positions as physicians, researchers, and executives. However, women still face challenges such as gender bias and unequal pay. Empowering women in health and wellness requires addressing these challenges and providing women with equal opportunities to succeed.

In conclusion, empowering women in leadership positions is crucial for creating a more equitable workplace and society. We need to challenge gender stereotypes and biases, support women's career advancement, and provide women with the resources and opportunities they need to succeed. By doing so, we can create a better world for everyone.

Creating a Gender-Inclusive Workplace

Creating a gender-inclusive workplace is essential for promoting diversity and inclusivity in the workplace. A gender-inclusive workplace is one that is welcoming to all genders, and it is essential to create an atmosphere that is free of gender bias. Gender bias can be subtle or overt, and it can impact the workplace in many ways. It can lead to a lack of diversity in the workplace, which can hinder productivity, creativity, and innovation.

To create a gender-inclusive workplace, it is important to first recognize and address any gender biases that may exist within the organization. This can be achieved through diversity training, which can help employees understand the importance of diversity and the negative impact of gender bias on the workplace.

Another way to create a gender-inclusive workplace is to promote gender diversity in leadership roles. This can be achieved by implementing policies that promote gender diversity in leadership positions, such as creating a gender-balanced hiring process or implementing a mentorship program for women. This can help to break down the barriers that women face in the workplace and create a more inclusive environment.

Additionally, it is essential to provide equal opportunities for both men and women in the workplace. This includes providing equal pay, equal opportunities for promotion, and equal access to training and development programs. By providing equal opportunities, the workplace can become more inclusive and diverse.

In conclusion, creating a gender-inclusive workplace is essential for promoting diversity and inclusivity in the workplace. It is important to recognize and address any gender biases that may exist within the organization, promote gender diversity in leadership roles, and provide equal opportunities for both men and women. By doing so, the workplace can become a more productive, innovative, and inclusive environment for all employees.

Empowering Women in Sports

Barriers faced by Women in Sports

Sports have traditionally been considered a male-dominated arena. However, women's participation in sports has gradually increased over the years. Despite this progress, women still face a number of barriers in sports that prevent them from fulfilling their full potential. In this subchapter, we will explore some of the key barriers faced by women in sports.

One of the main barriers faced by women in sports is a lack of funding and resources. Many women's sports teams receive little to no funding, which makes it difficult for them to compete at the highest level. This lack of funding also means that women's sports are often not broadcasted on television, which limits their exposure and opportunities for sponsorship.

Another major barrier is a lack of representation and recognition. Women's sports are often overshadowed by men's sports in the media, which means that female athletes receive less recognition and support. This lack of representation also means that women's sports are not taken as seriously as men's sports, which can lead to a lack of investment and resources.

sexism and discrimination are also major barriers faced by women in sports. Female athletes are often subjected to sexist comments and harassment, both sides on and off the field. This type of discrimination can make it difficult for women to feel comfortable and confident in their sports, and can also limit their opportunities for advancement.

Finally, women in sports often face a double standard when it comes to their appearance. Female athletes are expected to be attractive and feminine, which can be a distraction from their athletic abilities. This double standard can also lead to a lack of respect for female athletes and can limit their opportunities for endorsement deals and sponsorships.

In conclusion, women in sports face a number of barriers that prevent them from reaching their full potential. These barriers include a lack of funding and resources, a lack of representation and recognition, sexism and discrimination, and a double standard when it comes to appearance. It is important for us to recognize these barriers and work towards creating a more equal and inclusive sports environment for women.

The Importance of Female Role Models in Sports

Sports have long been considered a male-dominated field, but women are making strides in breaking down barriers and achieving greatness in various sports. Female athletes have been making headlines for their impressive performances, but they are not just making waves in the sports world. They are also inspiring women and girls everywhere to pursue their dreams in all areas of life. This is why female role models in sports are so crucial.

Female role models in sports provide a source of inspiration and motivation for women and girls who want to pursue sports or any other male-dominated field. They show that with hard work, determination, and perseverance, women can achieve anything they set their minds to. They also serve as a reminder that women can be just as strong, skilled, and successful as men.`

Moreover, female role models in sports can also have a positive impact on women's health and wellness. These women encourage women and girls to be physically active and take care of their bodies. They promote the importance of fitness, healthy eating, and self-care. By doing so, they help to combat the negative stereotypes that women face regarding their bodies and their physical abilities.

Female role models in sports also play a crucial role in empowering women in the workplace. They serve as a reminder that women can be leaders, innovators, and change-makers in any industry. They encourage women to break down barriers, speak up for themselves, and pursue their goals with confidence. They also provide a source of inspiration for women who want to break into male-dominated fields where women are underrepresented.

In conclusion, female role models in sports are essential in empowering women in all areas of life. They inspire women to pursue their dreams, promote health and wellness, and encourage women to break down barriers in the workplace. By celebrating and supporting female athletes, we can create a more inclusive and equitable society where women can thrive and achieve their full potential.

Bridging the Gender Pay Gap in Sports

Sports have long been considered a male-dominated field, with men often receiving higher pay and better opportunities than their female counterparts. However, in recent years, there has been a growing movement to bridge the gender pay gap in sports and ensure that women are treated fairly and equally.

One of the most significant challenges facing women in sports is the lack of investment and sponsorship. Many female athletes struggle to secure the funding they need to train and compete at the highest level, while male athletes often receive generous financial support from their sponsors.

To address this issue, initiatives like the Women's Sports Foundation have been working to increase funding for women's sports and promote equal opportunities for female athletes. Through programs like grants and scholarships, they are helping to level the playing field and ensure that women have the resources they need to succeed.

Another key factor in bridging the gender pay gap in sports is increasing visibility and representation for women. This means not only providing opportunities for female athletes to compete at the highest level but also ensuring that they are given equal coverage and recognition in the media.

To achieve this, it is essential to challenge the traditional gender roles and stereotypes that have long been perpetuated in sports. By promoting a more inclusive and diverse vision of what it means to be an athlete, we can help to break down barriers and create a more equitable playing field for all.

Ultimately, bridging the gender pay gap in sports requires a collaborative effort from all stakeholders, including athletes, coaches, sponsors, and fans. By working together to promote equality and empower women in sports, we can create a more just and inclusive world for all.

The Future of Women in Sports

Women have come a long way in the world of sports. From being barred from participating in many sports to being at the top of their game, women have proven that they are as capable as men in sports. However, there is still a long way to go to achieve true gender equality in sports.

The future of women in sports is looking bright. More and more girls are participating in sports, thanks to the efforts of organizations that promote sports for girls. The Women's Sports Foundation, for example, has been working to advance the lives of girls and women throughout sports and physical activity. Their efforts have resulted in more girls participating in sports, which is a positive trend for the future of women in sports.

One of the biggest challenges facing women in sports is the lack of media coverage. Men's sports receive far more coverage than women's sports, which makes it difficult for female athletes to gain recognition and opportunities. However, there have been some positive changes in recent years. With the rise of social media, female athletes have been able to gain a following and build their brand. This has helped to increase their visibility and attract sponsors.

Another challenge facing women in sports is the gender pay gap. Female athletes are often paid less than their male counterparts, even when they are performing at the same level. This is a problem that needs to be addressed if we want to achieve true gender equality in sports.

The future of women in sports also depends on the efforts of coaches, administrators, and other leaders in the sports world. They need to be committed to promoting gender equality and creating opportunities for women to succeed in sports. This includes providing equal funding for women's sports programs and ensuring that female athletes have access to the same resources and training as male athletes.

In conclusion, the future of women in sports is looking bright, but there is still a long way to go to achieve true gender equality. We need to continue to promote sports for girls, increase media coverage of women's sports, address the gender pay gap, and ensure that women have access to the same opportunities and resources as men. With these efforts, we can empower women in sports and create a more equal and inclusive world.

Empowering Women in Politics

Women have come a long way in politics, but they still face many barriers. Despite the fact that women make up more than half of the population, they are still greatly underrepresented in political positions. Women make up only a small percentage of elected officials, and they often face sexism and discrimination when trying to enter the political arena.

One of the biggest barriers faced by women in politics is the lack of support and resources available to them. Women often have to work harder than men to gain the same level of recognition and support, and they may not have access to the same networks and resources as male candidates.

Another barrier faced by women in politics is the gender bias that exists in many political institutions. Women are often viewed as less competent or less qualified than their male counterparts, and they may be overlooked for leadership positions or important committee assignments.

Sexual harassment and discrimination are also major barriers faced by women in politics. Women who speak out against harassment or discrimination may be labeled as troublemakers or risk losing key support.

Finally, women often face the challenge of balancing their political careers with their family responsibilities. Women are often expected to prioritize their roles as wives and mothers over their political ambitions, and they may struggle to find the time and resources necessary to pursue a career in politics.

Despite these barriers, there are many ways that women can break through and succeed in politics. Women can seek out mentors and support networks, work to build their skills and experience, and advocate for policies that support gender equality and women's rights.

In order to truly empower women in politics, we must work to dismantle the gender bias and discrimination that exists in our political institutions. We must also work to create more opportunities for women to enter politics and ensure that they have the resources and support they need to succeed.

By breaking down these barriers, we can create a more equitable and inclusive political system that truly represents the diversity of our population. With more women in politics, we can create a brighter and more prosperous future for all.

The Importance of Women in Politics

Women have played a vital role in shaping society, and their presence in leadership positions is critical to promoting gender equality and ensuring that the needs and interests of women are represented and addressed. Women in politics have a unique opportunity to influence policy and decision-making on issues such as education, health care, and gender-based violence, among others.

Despite significant progress over the years, women are still underrepresented in political leadership positions globally. According to the Inter-Parliamentary Union, women make up only 25% of parliamentarians worldwide. This gender imbalance not only undermines democracy but also limits the potential impact of policies that could benefit women and girls.

The importance of women in politics cannot be overstated. Women can bring a different perspective to the policymaking process, one that is grounded in their lived experiences and the realities of their communities. This perspective can help to identify and address issues that may be overlooked by male politicians.

Moreover, women in politics can serve as role models for young women and girls, inspiring them to pursue leadership positions and aspire to greatness. They can help to break down stereotypes and push for greater gender equality in all spheres of society.

Empowering women in politics requires a concerted effort to address the barriers that prevent women from entering and thriving in political leadership positions. This includes addressing gender-based discrimination, promoting women's political participation, and providing support and mentorship to women who aspire to be political leaders.

In conclusion, the importance of women in politics cannot be overemphasized. Women bring a unique perspective to the policymaking process that is critical to promoting gender equality and ensuring that the needs and interests of women are represented and addressed. Empowering women in politics requires a collective effort to address the barriers that prevent women from entering and thriving in political leadership positions. It is time to break down the gender barriers and create an inclusive political system that reflects the diversity of our society.

Creating a More Gender-Inclusive Political System

Politics has long been dominated by men, but there is a growing movement to create a more gender-inclusive political system. Women are underrepresented in political leadership positions, and this has negative effects on the policies and decisions made by our governments.

Empowering women in politics is crucial to creating a more equitable and just society. Women bring unique perspectives and experiences to the table, and their voices must be heard.

However, there are many barriers that prevent women from entering politics and rising to leadership positions.

One of the biggest barriers is the lack of support and resources available to women. Political campaigns are expensive, and women often have less access to financial resources than men. Additionally, women face sexist and discriminatory attitudes from both voters and other politicians.

To create a more gender-inclusive political system, we must address these barriers and provide more support and resources to women. This includes providing funding for women's political campaigns, implementing policies to combat sexism and discrimination in politics, and promoting women's leadership in politics.

We must also prioritize the recruitment and training of women for political leadership positions. This means providing mentorship and coaching programs for women interested in politics, as well as creating more opportunities for women to gain experience and build their skills.

Finally, we must work to change the cultural attitudes and norms that hold women back in politics. This means challenging sexist and discriminatory beliefs and promoting gender equality in all aspects of society.

Creating a more gender-inclusive political system is not only important for women's empowerment, but for the well-being of our society as a whole. When women are empowered in politics, they bring new perspectives, ideas, and solutions to the table, leading to more effective and equitable policies and decision-making.

The Future of Women in Politics

It is no secret that women have been underrepresented in politics for decades. However, in recent years, we have seen a surge of women entering the political arena and making history. In 2019, a record-breaking 127 women were elected to the United States Congress, and Kamala Harris became the first woman, as well as the first person of color, to be elected Vice President of the United States. These victories are a testament to the progress that women have made in politics, but there is still much work to be done.

The future of women in politics is bright. As more and more women enter the political arena, they are bringing their unique perspectives and experiences to the table. Women are more likely to prioritize issues such as healthcare, education, and equal pay, which are often overlooked by their male counterparts. By electing more women to public office, we can create a more diverse and representative government that truly reflects the needs and desires of the people.

However, women still face significant barriers in politics. They are often subjected to sexist attacks and discrimination, which can deter them from running for office. Women are also less likely to receive the financial support and endorsements necessary to run a successful campaign. These obstacles must be addressed if we want to see more women in political leadership positions.

Empowering women in politics starts with encouraging them to run for office. Women need to be supported and encouraged to pursue their political ambitions, whether that means running for city council or running for president. We also need to ensure that women have access to the resources and networks necessary to run successful campaigns. This includes financial support, mentorship programs, and training on how to navigate the political landscape.

In addition, we need to address the systemic barriers that prevent women from succeeding in politics. This includes increasing representation in leadership positions and implementing policies that promote gender equity. We also need to hold politicians and political parties accountable for their actions and ensure that they are actively working to promote gender equality.

The future of women in politics is bright, but it is up to all of us to ensure that women are empowered to lead. By supporting women in politics, we can create a more inclusive and representative government that truly reflects the needs and desires of all citizens.

Empowering Women in Education

Barriers faced by Women in Education

Education is the foundation of any society, and it is essential for the development of every individual. However, women have faced several barriers in accessing education for centuries. Although there have been significant improvements in recent years, we cannot deny that women still face obstacles in education.

One of the main barriers faced by women in education is gender bias. Societal beliefs and stereotypes about women have led to discrimination in educational settings. Women often face discrimination in their access to education, the quality of education provided to them, and the opportunities for growth and development that are available to them.

Another significant barrier is cultural and social norms. Many cultures still view women as the primary caretakers of the home, which means that education often takes a back seat for women. Some societies still believe that educating women is a waste of resources since they will eventually leave their homes to get married and raise children.

Additionally, poverty is a significant factor that affects women's access to education. Girls from low-income families often do not have access to quality education due to the inability to pay for school fees, uniforms, and other basic necessities needed for education. This lack of access to education can lead to a cycle of poverty that can last for generations.

Harassment and violence against women in educational settings is also a significant barrier. Women and girls are often subjected to sexual harassment, assault, and violence in schools and universities. This abuse can have long-lasting effects on women's physical and mental health, and it can lead to a lack of motivation to continue their education.

In conclusion, women face several barriers that hinder their access to education. These barriers include gender bias, cultural and social norms, poverty, and harassment. As a society, we must work to eliminate these barriers and provide equal opportunities for women to access quality education. By doing so, we can empower women to reach their full potential in all niches, including entrepreneurship, leadership, technology, finance, arts, health and wellness, politics, sports, and the workplace.

The Importance of Women in Education

The importance of women in education cannot be overstated. Education is the foundation for personal and professional growth, and it is essential in empowering women to achieve their goals. By providing women with access to education, we are not only empowering them but also the communities and societies in which they live.

Empowering women in education has a ripple effect that extends beyond the individual. Educated women are more likely to have healthier families, participate in the workforce, and make informed decisions about their lives. They are also better equipped to advocate for their own rights, the rights of their communities, and the rights of other women.

Unfortunately, access to education is still a significant challenge for many women, particularly in developing countries. This is due to various factors such as poverty, cultural norms, and lack of infrastructure. As a result, many women are denied the opportunity to learn and realize their full potential.

One way to empower women in education is to invest in girls' education. Studies have shown that educating girls has a significant impact on economic development, as educated women are more likely to contribute to the workforce and generate income. It also leads to better health outcomes for mothers and children, as educated women are more likely to have access to healthcare and make informed decisions about their families' well-being.

Another way to empower women in education is to promote gender equality in schools and universities. This includes ensuring equal access to resources and opportunities, as well as creating a safe and inclusive learning environment free from discrimination and harassment.

In conclusion, empowering women in education is crucial in promoting gender equality and creating a more just and equitable society. By investing in girls' education and promoting gender equality in schools and universities, we can break down barriers and provide women with the tools they need to succeed in all aspects of life. It is time for us all to recognize the importance of women in education and take action to ensure that every woman has access to the education she deserves.

Creating a More Gender-Inclusive Education System

In today's world, we need to ensure that we create a more gender-inclusive education system. This is because education is the key to unlocking the potential of individuals and society as a whole. It is essential that we provide equal opportunities for men and women to learn and grow, without any biases or discrimination. In this subchapter, we will explore how we can create a more gender-inclusive education system that empowers women and prepares them for success in all areas of life.

Firstly, we need to address the gender bias that exists in textbooks, curriculums, and teaching methods. Many textbooks and curriculums are biased towards men, and this often results in girls being excluded or discouraged from pursuing certain subjects. Additionally, teaching methods that favor one gender over the other can also have a negative impact on learning outcomes. To address this issue, we need to ensure that textbooks and curriculums are gender-neutral, and teaching methods are inclusive of both genders.

Another crucial aspect of creating a more gender-inclusive education system is to provide equal opportunities for girls and women in all areas of education. This includes providing access to quality education, scholarships, and encouraging girls to pursue STEM (Science, Technology, Engineering, and Mathematics) fields that are traditionally male-dominated. By providing equal opportunities, we can empower women to break barriers and achieve their full potential.

Lastly, we need to focus on developing a culture of respect and tolerance in our schools and universities. This means creating a safe and inclusive environment where students can learn and grow without fear of discrimination or harassment. By promoting a culture of respect and tolerance, we can help women feel more comfortable and confident in pursuing their education, careers, and other areas of life.

In conclusion, creating a more gender-inclusive education system is essential for empowering women and preparing them for success in all areas of life. By addressing gender bias in textbooks, providing equal opportunities, and promoting a culture of respect and tolerance, we can create a more inclusive education system that benefits everyone. Let us work together to break barriers and empower women in education and beyond.

The Future of Women in Education

Education is a fundamental tool for the empowerment of women. It has the power to change the lives of individuals, families, and communities. However, the journey towards gender equality in education has not been smooth. In many parts of the world, women and girls still face significant barriers to access quality education. Despite progress made in recent years, the future of women in education remains uncertain.

One of the biggest challenges facing women in education is the persistent gender gap. According to UNESCO, there are still 132 million girls out of school globally, and 15 million girls of primary-school age may never get the chance to learn to read or write. This gender gap is even more pronounced in developing countries, where cultural and economic barriers prevent girls from accessing education.

Another challenge is the underrepresentation of women in leadership roles in education. Women make up the majority of teachers, but they are significantly underrepresented in higher education leadership positions. According to a report by the American Council on Education, women occupy only 30% of college and university presidencies. This lack of representation can limit the perspectives and experiences that shape educational policies and practices.

Despite these challenges, there is reason for optimism. The rise of technology has created new opportunities for women in education. Online learning platforms and digital resources can help bridge the gender gap and provide access to education for women and girls in remote areas.

Moreover, there is a growing recognition of the importance of gender equality in education. Governments, non-governmental organizations, and educational institutions are increasingly focused on promoting gender-sensitive policies and practices. There is also a growing movement towards empowering women and girls as agents of change in their communities.

To ensure a bright future for women in education, it is crucial to continue to promote policies and practices that support gender equality. This includes addressing the underlying social, cultural, and economic barriers that prevent women and girls from accessing education. It also means promoting women's leadership and representation in education and investing in technology and digital resources that can help bridge the gender gap.

In conclusion, the future of women in education is both challenging and promising. While there is still much work to be done to ensure gender equality in education, there is also growing recognition of the importance of empowering women and girls as agents of change. By working together, we can create a world where every woman and girl has access to quality education and the opportunity to reach her full potential.

Empowering Women in Entrepreneurship

Challenges Faced by Women in Entrepreneurship

Women have made remarkable strides in the world of entrepreneurship, breaking down barriers and paving the way for a new generation of female leaders. However, despite these achievements, women in entrepreneurship still face a number of challenges that men do not have to contend with. In this subchapter, we will examine the challenges faced by women in entrepreneurship, from discrimination to limited access to funding, and explore ways to overcome them.

One of the biggest challenges faced by women in entrepreneurship is discrimination. Women often have to work twice as hard as men to prove themselves in a male-dominated industry. They are frequently subjected to gender bias, often being overlooked for leadership positions or funding opportunities. This can lead to a lack of visibility and opportunities for women entrepreneurs, making it harder for them to succeed.

Another major challenge faced by women in entrepreneurship is a lack of access to funding. Women entrepreneurs often have a harder time securing investment capital than their male counterparts. According to a report by PitchBook, only 2.3% of venture capital funding went to female-led startups in 2020. This disparity is not only unfair, but it also limits the potential for growth and innovation in the industry.

Women entrepreneurs also face unique challenges when it comes to balancing work and family life. Many women are still expected to take on the bulk of caregiving responsibilities, which can make it difficult to devote the time and energy needed to run a successful business. This can lead to burnout and a lack of work-life balance, which can be detrimental to both the entrepreneur and the business.

Despite these challenges, women in entrepreneurship have shown remarkable resilience and determination. They have created their own networks and support systems, and have found ways to overcome the obstacles they face. By continuing to advocate for greater diversity and inclusion in the industry, and by supporting and mentoring the next generation of women entrepreneurs, we can create a more equitable and inclusive entrepreneurial landscape for all.

The Importance of Women in Entrepreneurship

Entrepreneurship is a field that has traditionally been dominated by men. However, in recent years, women have been breaking barriers and making tremendous strides in this arena. The importance of women in entrepreneurship cannot be overstated. Not only does their presence bring diversity and innovation to the field, but it also helps to drive economic growth and create jobs.

When women are empowered to start and run their own businesses, it has a ripple effect in their communities and beyond. Women entrepreneurs are more likely to hire other women, which helps to close the gender pay gap and create opportunities for women who may have otherwise been overlooked in the job market. In addition, women-led businesses tend to be more socially conscious and environmentally friendly, which has a positive impact on the planet and society as a whole.

Empowering women in entrepreneurship is not just important from an economic standpoint, but also from a social and cultural one. When women are given the tools and resources they need to succeed as entrepreneurs, they are able to challenge gender norms and break down barriers that have held them back for far too long. This not only benefits individual women, but it also helps to create a more equal and just society for all.

If we want to see real progress towards gender equality, we need to support and encourage women in entrepreneurship. This means providing access to funding, mentorship, and training programs that can help women develop the skills and knowledge they need to succeed. It also means changing cultural attitudes and biases that have historically held women back from pursuing careers in entrepreneurship.

In conclusion, the importance of women in entrepreneurship cannot be overstated. Women bring diversity, innovation, and social consciousness to the field, and their success has a positive impact on the economy, society, and culture as a whole. By supporting and empowering women in entrepreneurship, we can create a more equal and just world for all.

Creating a More Gender-Inclusive Entrepreneurship Ecosystem

Entrepreneurship is an essential element of any economy. It is a driving force behind innovation, job creation, and economic growth. However, the reality is that women face significant challenges in accessing the resources and support necessary for starting and scaling their businesses. In this subchapter, we will explore the barriers that women entrepreneurs face, and provide actionable steps to create a more gender-inclusive entrepreneurship ecosystem.

The Challenges Women Entrepreneurs Face

Women entrepreneurs face a range of challenges that limit their ability to start and grow their businesses. These challenges include:

1. Access to Capital: Women entrepreneurs face significant barriers in accessing the capital necessary to start and scale their businesses. Studies have shown that women receive less funding than men, even when controlling for factors such as industry, experience, and education.

2. Networking: Women tend to have smaller networks than men, which limits their ability to access resources such as funding, mentorship, and business opportunities.

3. Stereotypes and Bias: Women face stereotypes and bias in the entrepreneurship ecosystem, which can limit their access to resources and opportunities. This bias can come in the form of assumptions about women's abilities, lack of representation in key decision-making positions, and gendered language in entrepreneurship discourse.

4. Work-Life Balance: Women are more likely to have caregiving responsibilities, which can limit their ability to devote time and resources to their businesses.

Steps to Create a More Gender-Inclusive Entrepreneurship Ecosystem

1. Increase Access to Capital: To create a more gender-inclusive entrepreneurship ecosystem, we must increase access to capital for women entrepreneurs. This can be achieved through initiatives such as:

   a. Government funding programs that prioritize women-led businesses.

   b. Investment funds that focus on funding women-led businesses.

   c. Corporate social responsibility initiatives that support women entrepreneurs.

2. Expand Networks: Another critical step is to expand women's networks by creating opportunities for women to connect with mentors, investors, and other entrepreneurs. This can be achieved through initiatives such as:

   a. Women-focused networking events and conferences.

   b. Mentorship programs that connect women entrepreneurs with experienced mentors.

   c. Online communities and forums that allow women to connect and share resources.

3. Address Stereotypes and Bias: To create a more gender-inclusive entrepreneurship ecosystem, we must also address

stereotypes and bias. This can be achieved through initiatives such as:

    a. Education and training programs that promote gender-neutral language and challenge gender stereotypes.

    b. Diversity and inclusion initiatives that promote the representation of women in key decision- making positions.

    c. Awareness campaigns that highlight the contributions of women entrepreneurs.

4. Support Work-Life Balance: Finally, we must support women entrepreneurs' work-life balance by providing access to resources such as:

    a. Childcare services.

    b. Flexible work arrangements.

    c. Time-management training.

Conclusion

Creating a more gender-inclusive entrepreneurship ecosystem is essential for unlocking the full potential of women entrepreneurs. By increasing access to capital, expanding networks, addressing stereotypes and bias, and supporting work-life balance, we can create an environment that empowers women to start and scale their businesses. By doing so, we can drive innovation, job creation, and economic growth, benefiting not only women entrepreneurs but society as a whole.

The Future of Women in Entrepreneurship

Entrepreneurship has always been a male-dominated field. However, times have changed, and women have slowly but surely made their mark in the business world. The future of women in entrepreneurship looks promising, and here's why.

Firstly, women are breaking down the barriers that have held them back in the past. They are starting their own businesses and taking on leadership roles in existing ones. According to a report by American Express, women started an average of 1,821 new businesses per day in the United States in 2019. This goes to show that women are no longer afraid to take risks and pursue their dreams.

Secondly, technology has given women a platform to showcase their talents and ideas. Social media and e-commerce have made it easier for women to start and grow their businesses. They can now reach a wider audience and sell their products and services online. This has levelled the playing field for women entrepreneurs and given them more opportunities to succeed.

Thirdly, the pandemic has forced many women to pivot and come up with innovative solutions to keep their businesses afloat. They have had to be creative and adaptable in the face of challenges. This resilience and resourcefulness will serve them well in the future.

However, there are still challenges that women face in entrepreneurship. One of the biggest hurdles is access to funding. Women-owned businesses receive only a fraction of the venture capital that men do. This is why it's important for investors and financial institutions to recognize the potential of women-led businesses and provide them with the necessary support.

Another challenge is the lack of representation and mentorship for women in entrepreneurship. This is where women leaders and successful entrepreneurs can step in and serve as role models and mentors for the next generation of women entrepreneurs.

In conclusion, the future of women in entrepreneurship is bright. Women are breaking barriers, leveraging technology and showing resilience in the face of challenges. With the right support and opportunities, women can continue to make significant contributions to the business world and inspire other women to do the same.

Empowering Women in Leadership

Barriers Faced by Women in Leadership

In today's world, women have made significant strides in various fields, including education, sports, politics, entrepreneurship, and technology. However, when it comes to leadership positions, women are still underrepresented and face various barriers that prevent them from reaching their full potential. This subchapter will explore some of the most common obstacles that women face in leadership positions.

One of the most significant barriers that women face in leadership is gender bias and stereotypes. Despite the progress made towards gender equality, many people still believe that men are better suited for leadership positions than women. As a result, women are often overlooked for promotions and leadership roles, even if they are equally qualified or more qualified than their male counterparts. This bias can also manifest in subtle ways, such as assuming that women are less assertive or less competent than men.

Another barrier that women face in leadership is the lack of support and mentorship. Many women report feeling isolated and unsupported in their leadership roles, which can make it challenging to navigate the workplace and advance their careers. Women often lack access to the same networks and opportunities as men, which can limit their ability to build relationships and gain visibility within their organizations.

Work-life balance is another significant barrier that women face in leadership. Many women struggle to balance their professional responsibilities with their personal lives, especially if they have children or other caregiving responsibilities. The lack of flexible work arrangements and support for working parents can make it challenging for women to advance their careers while also meeting their family obligations.

Finally, women often face a lack of representation in leadership positions. When there are no women in leadership roles, it can be challenging to envision oneself in those positions, and it can also reinforce the idea that women are not capable of leading. This lack of representation can also make it challenging for women to find mentors and role models who can help guide them in their careers.

In conclusion, women face many barriers in leadership positions, including gender bias and stereotypes, lack of support and mentorship, work-life balance challenges, and lack of representation. It is essential to recognize these barriers and work towards creating more inclusive and equitable workplaces where women can thrive and reach their full potential. By empowering women in leadership, we can create a more diverse and effective workforce that benefits everyone.

The Importance of Women in Leadership

Women have always been an integral part of society, and their presence in leadership roles is crucial for a better future. Women bring a unique perspective and approach to leadership, which is often different from that of men. Women leaders are empathetic, compassionate, and nurturing, and they tend to focus more on teamwork and collaboration rather than competition and dominance.

Empowering women in leadership is crucial for the growth and development of any organization. Women leaders bring diversity to the table, which leads to a broader range of ideas and perspectives. This diversity helps in decision-making and problem-solving, leading to better outcomes for the organization.

Women in leadership positions also serve as role models for other women, encouraging them to aspire to leadership roles. When women see other women in leadership positions, they become more confident in their abilities and are more likely to pursue leadership roles themselves.

Empowering women in leadership is also essential for achieving gender equality. Women have historically been underrepresented in leadership positions, and this has led to the perpetuation of gender inequality. By empowering women in leadership, we can break down these barriers and create a more equitable society.

Women in leadership positions can also help to address issues that disproportionately affect women, such as gender-based violence and discrimination in the workplace. Women leaders can use their positions of power to advocate for policies that promote gender equality and to create safe and inclusive work environments.

In conclusion, empowering women in leadership is essential for the growth and development of any organization and for achieving gender equality. Women leaders bring unique perspectives and approaches to leadership, which leads to better decision-making and problem-solving.

They also serve as role models for other women, encouraging them to aspire to leadership roles. It is time to break down the barriers that prevent women from reaching their full potential and to empower women in leadership roles across all industries.

Creating a More Gender-Inclusive Leadership Ecosystem

A gender-inclusive leadership ecosystem is one in which men and women have equal opportunities and support to rise to leadership positions in their respective fields. However, this system is not yet fully established in many industries and sectors. Women continue to face barriers that prevent them from attaining leadership positions, and this affects not only their personal growth but also the growth and success of the organizations they belong to.

To create a more gender-inclusive leadership ecosystem, we must first acknowledge the existing biases and stereotypes that hinder women's progress. We need to address the unconscious biases that prevent women from being seen as capable leaders and challenge the gender stereotypes that limit their potential. This means actively seeking out and promoting women for leadership positions, providing them with the necessary training and support to succeed, and breaking down the barriers that prevent them from advancing.

One way to create a more gender-inclusive leadership ecosystem is by implementing policies and programs that promote gender diversity. This includes setting diversity targets and tracking progress, providing leadership training and mentorship programs for women, and encouraging flexible work arrangements that support work-life balance.

It is also essential to create safe and inclusive spaces for women to share their experiences and challenges. This includes providing opportunities for women to network and connect with other women in their field, as well as creating support groups and forums for women to discuss topics such as gender bias and discrimination.

Finally, it is crucial to have men as allies in the fight for gender equality. Men can play a significant role in promoting gender diversity by educating themselves and others about gender bias and discrimination, advocating for gender-inclusive policies and practices, and actively supporting and promoting women in leadership positions.

In conclusion, creating a more gender-inclusive leadership ecosystem requires a concerted effort from both men and women. By acknowledging and addressing existing biases and stereotypes, implementing diversity policies and programs, creating safe and inclusive spaces for women, and having men as allies, we can create a more equitable and successful work environment for everyone.

The Future of Women in Leadership

The future of women in leadership is bright, but there is still much work to be done to ensure that women have equal opportunities to lead in all areas of society. Empowering women in the workplace, sports, politics, education, entrepreneurship, technology, finance, the arts, and health and wellness is essential for creating a more equitable and just world.

In the workplace, women are still underrepresented in leadership positions. According to a study by McKinsey & Company, women make up only 38% of first-level managers and just 22% of C-suite executives. This is despite the fact that companies with more diverse leadership teams tend to be more profitable and innovative. To increase the number of women in leadership roles, companies must actively work to eliminate bias in hiring and promotion processes, provide mentorship and sponsorship opportunities, and offer flexible work arrangements that allow women to balance work and family responsibilities.

In sports, women have made significant strides in recent years, but there is still a long way to go. Women's sports are often given less media coverage and fewer resources than men's sports, and female athletes are paid significantly less than their male counterparts. To empower women in sports, we must invest in girls' sports programs and provide equal resources and opportunities for female athletes. We must also challenge stereotypes and biases that limit girls' and women's participation in sports.

In politics, women are underrepresented at all levels of government. While women make up more than half of the population, they hold only 24% of seats in national parliaments worldwide. To empower women in politics, we must encourage more women to run for office, provide training and support for female candidates, and challenge gender-based stereotypes and biases that limit women's political participation.

In education, empowering women means ensuring that girls have access to quality education and are encouraged to pursue their passions and interests. It also means challenging gender- based stereotypes and biases that limit girls' and women's educational and career opportunities.

In entrepreneurship, empowering women means providing access to funding, mentorship, and resources that can help female entrepreneurs start and grow successful businesses. It also means challenging gender-based biases and stereotypes that limit women's access to capital and other resources.

In technology, empowering women means increasing the number of women in technology- related fields and ensuring that they have equal access to opportunities for advancement and leadership. It also means challenging gender-based biases and stereotypes that limit women's participation in technology.

In finance, empowering women means ensuring that women have equal access to financial resources and opportunities for investment and wealth creation. It also means challenging gender-based biases and stereotypes that limit women's access to financial services and opportunities.

In the arts, empowering women means providing equal opportunities for female artists and challenging gender-based biases and stereotypes that limit women's artistic expression and opportunities for success.

In health and wellness, empowering women means providing access to quality healthcare and resources that can help women lead healthy and fulfilling lives. It also means challenging gender- based biases and stereotypes that limit women's access to healthcare and opportunities for wellness.

In conclusion, empowering women in leadership is essential for creating a more equitable and just world. To achieve this goal, we must challenge gender-based biases and stereotypes, provide equal opportunities and resources, and encourage women to pursue their passions and interests. By doing so, we can create a world where women are able to lead and succeed in all areas of society.

Empowering Women in Technology

Challenges Faced by Women in Technology

Despite the progress made in terms of gender equality, women still face challenges in the technology industry. The tech industry is known for being male-dominated, and this can make it difficult for women to break in and succeed. Here are some of the challenges that women in technology face:

1. Gender Bias: One of the biggest challenges that women face in the technology industry is gender bias. Women are often viewed as less capable than men, and this bias can impact their ability to advance in their careers. Women may also face discrimination when it comes to hiring, promotions, and pay.

2. Lack of Female Role Models: When there are few women in leadership positions, it can be difficult for other women to envision themselves in those roles. Without female role models, it can be hard for women to see a path forward in their careers.

3. Work-Life Balance: Many women in technology struggle to balance their work and personal lives. Long hours and high-pressure environments can make it challenging to maintain a healthy work-life balance, and this can impact women's ability to

advance in their careers.

4. Lack of Support: Women in technology may not receive the same level of support as their male counterparts. This can include things like mentorship, networking opportunities, and access to resources. Without this support, it can be difficult for women to succeed in the industry.

5. Stereotypes: Women in technology may face stereotypes about their abilities and interests. Some people assume that women are not interested in technical work or that they are not as capable as men in this field. These stereotypes can be damaging and can make it harder for women to succeed.

Despite these challenges, women in technology are making progress. More and more women are entering the industry and breaking down barriers. By supporting and empowering women in technology, we can help to create a more diverse and inclusive industry that benefits everyone.

The Importance of Women in Technology

Technology is one of the fastest growing industries in the world, and it is crucial that women play a significant role in its development. The tech industry has historically been male-dominated, but this trend is changing rapidly. Women are breaking barriers in technology and making significant contributions to the industry.

Women bring unique perspectives and ideas to the table, which is essential in developing innovative technology. Studies have shown that diverse teams lead to better decision-making and more creative solutions. Having women in technology roles ensures that different perspectives are represented, leading to more successful outcomes.

Encouraging women to pursue careers in technology is also crucial for gender equality. Women are still underrepresented in STEM fields, and this gap needs to be closed. By empowering women in technology, we can create more opportunities for young girls to see themselves in these roles and strive to pursue them.

Additionally, women in technology can serve as role models for future generations. Seeing successful women in technology can inspire young girls to pursue careers in STEM fields and break down gender barriers in the industry. It is important for women in technology to mentor and support younger women, creating a pipeline of talent for the future.

The tech industry is constantly evolving, and it is essential that women have a seat at the table. By including women in the development and creation of technology, we can ensure that products and services are designed with diversity and inclusivity in mind. This will lead to a better user experience for all, regardless of gender, race, or background.

In conclusion, women are essential in the tech industry and should be encouraged to pursue careers in technology. By empowering women in technology, we can create a more diverse and inclusive industry, leading to better outcomes for all. Women in technology can serve as role models and mentors, inspiring future generations to pursue careers in STEM fields. Let us break down gender barriers in technology and work towards a more equitable and inclusive future.

Creating a More Gender-Inclusive Technology Ecosystem

The technology industry has been long criticized for its lack of gender diversity. Women are underrepresented in this field, and this has led to a lack of perspective and a lack of innovation. However, the good news is that organizations and individuals are now working towards creating a more gender-inclusive technology ecosystem. This chapter will discuss ways in which we can create a more gender-inclusive technology ecosystem.

Firstly, organizations must take the initiative to create a more gender-inclusive work environment. This can be achieved by providing equal opportunities for both genders, offering training and mentorship programs, and creating a culture of inclusiveness. Organizations must also ensure that they address any cases of sexism or harassment in the workplace, as this can be a major deterrent for women wanting to enter the industry.

Secondly, education plays a vital role in creating a more gender-inclusive technology ecosystem. There is a need to encourage girls and young women to pursue careers in technology. This can be achieved by providing them with access to technology programs and mentorship opportunities. By doing so, we can inspire young women to take up technology-related subjects and careers.

Thirdly, we need to support women-led startups and businesses. Women entrepreneurs face several challenges when starting a business, and this is especially true in the technology industry. Investors tend to be biased towards male-led startups, and this makes it difficult for women-led startups to secure funding. By supporting women-led startups, we can create a more gender- inclusive technology ecosystem.

Lastly, we need to change the way we think about technology. Gender stereotypes often lead to women being excluded from the technology industry. We need to challenge these stereotypes and create a culture that celebrates diversity and inclusiveness. This can be achieved by highlighting the achievements of women in technology and showcasing the impact that technology can have on society.

In conclusion, creating a more gender-inclusive technology ecosystem requires a concerted effort from organizations, individuals, and society as a whole. By taking the steps discussed in this chapter, we can create a more diverse and innovative technology industry, which will benefit everyone.

The Future of Women in Technology

Technology has been one of the fastest-growing industries in the world, and it is expected to continue to grow in the years to come. Despite this growth, women are still underrepresented in the tech industry. According to recent studies, women hold only 25% of IT jobs, and only 5% of tech startups are founded by women. This gender gap in technology is not only a problem for women, but it is also a problem for the industry as a whole.

The future of women in technology is bright, and it is up to everyone in the industry to work together to create a more inclusive and diverse workforce. One way to do this is to encourage young girls to pursue careers in technology. Many girls do not consider technology as a career option because they believe it is a male-dominated industry. It is essential to change this perception and show girls that they can succeed in technology.

Another way to increase the number of women in technology is to provide support and mentorship for women already in the industry. Many women face unique challenges in the tech industry, such as unconscious bias, lack of support, and a lack of female role models. Providing support and mentorship can help women overcome these challenges and succeed in their careers.

In addition, it is essential to create a culture of inclusion in the tech industry. This means creating a workplace where everyone feels valued and respected, regardless of their gender, race, or background. Companies need to address any biases that may exist and provide training for employees on how to be more inclusive.

The future of women in technology is not just about increasing the number of women in the industry. It is also about creating a more diverse and inclusive workforce that benefits everyone. Studies have shown that diverse teams are more innovative and productive. By increasing the number of women in technology, we can create a more innovative and productive industry.

In conclusion, the future of women in technology is bright, but there is still a lot of work to be done. We need to encourage young girls to pursue careers in technology, provide support and mentorship for women already in the industry, and create a culture of inclusion in the tech industry. By working together, we can create a more diverse and inclusive tech industry that benefits everyone.

Empowering Women in Finance

Barriers Faced by Women in Finance

Despite the progress that women have made in the financial industry, there are still significant barriers that prevent them from achieving full gender equality. Women make up just 23% of executive and senior-level positions in finance, and the gender pay gap in the industry remains significant. In this chapter, we will explore the barriers that women face in finance and discuss strategies for overcoming them.

One of the biggest barriers for women in finance is the lack of female role models and mentors. Women in finance often report feeling isolated and unsupported, which can make it difficult to advance in their careers. Additionally, women are often subject to gender bias and discrimination, which can result in lower salaries and fewer opportunities for advancement.

Another significant barrier for women in finance is the lack of flexible work arrangements.

Many women in finance are also caregivers, and the demands of the industry can make it difficult to balance work and family responsibilities. This can result in women being passed over for promotions or being forced to choose between their careers and their families.

Finally, there is a lack of diversity in the financial industry, which can make it difficult for women to feel included and valued. Women of color, in particular, face unique challenges in the industry, such as the stereotype of being too aggressive or assertive.

To address these barriers, there are several strategies that women in finance can employ. First, it is important to seek out female mentors and role models who can provide guidance and support.

Women can also advocate for themselves and negotiate for better salaries and opportunities for advancement. Additionally, companies can implement flexible work arrangements and policies that support work-life balance.

Finally, it is essential to promote diversity and inclusion in the financial industry. Companies can do this by recruiting and promoting women and people of color, creating a culture that values diversity, and providing training and resources to combat gender bias and discrimination.

In conclusion, while women have made significant progress in the financial industry, there are still significant barriers that prevent them from achieving full gender equality. By seeking out mentors, advocating for themselves, and promoting diversity and inclusion, women in finance can overcome these barriers and achieve success in their careers.

The Importance of Women in Finance

Finance has long been a male-dominated field, with women facing significant challenges in breaking through the glass ceiling. However, women are essential to the finance industry's success and play a critical role in driving innovation, growth, and profitability.

Women bring unique perspectives and skills to the finance industry. They are often more collaborative, empathetic, and intuitive than their male counterparts, making them excellent problem solvers and skilled negotiators. Women also tend to be more risk-averse, which can be an asset in the world of finance, where risk management is often a critical component of success.

Despite their value, women continue to face significant barriers in the finance industry. According to a recent study by the World Economic Forum, women account for just 21% of executive committee positions in the financial sector. This lack of representation not only limits women's career opportunities but also has a negative impact on the industry's bottom line.

Research shows that companies with diverse leadership teams are more innovative, have better financial performance, and are better equipped to manage risk. However, achieving gender diversity in finance requires a concerted effort from both men and women.

Men must become advocates for women in finance, working to eliminate the unconscious biases that often prevent women from advancing in their careers. This could involve challenging the status quo, promoting diverse hiring practices, and advocating for more women in leadership roles.

Women, on the other hand, must continue to push for change and take advantage of opportunities to break down barriers. This could involve seeking out mentors and sponsors, advocating for themselves, and pursuing education and training to develop their skills.

In conclusion, the finance industry needs women, and women need the finance industry. Achieving gender diversity is essential for the industry's success and will benefit everyone involved. By working together, we can break down barriers and create a more inclusive and equitable finance industry for all.

Creating a More Gender-Inclusive Finance Ecosystem

The world of finance traditionally has been a male-dominated industry. Women have been underrepresented in leadership positions, and they have faced barriers in access to capital, funding, and investment opportunities. However, the tide is turning, and there's a growing recognition that gender diversity in the finance ecosystem is essential for economic growth and social progress.

To create a more gender-inclusive finance ecosystem, we need to take a multi-pronged approach. Here are some strategies that can help:

1. Increase Women's Representation in Leadership Positions

One of the most critical steps in creating a more gender-inclusive finance ecosystem is to increase women's representation in leadership positions. Research has shown that companies with more women in leadership positions tend to be more profitable and innovative.

To achieve this, companies need to set targets and create policies that promote gender diversity and inclusion. They should also address unconscious biases in the hiring process and provide mentorship and sponsorship opportunities for women.

2. Provide Access to Capital and Funding Opportunities

Women entrepreneurs face significant challenges in accessing capital and funding opportunities. This is due in part to the lack of diversity in the venture capital industry, which is dominated by men. To address this issue, we need to create more opportunities for women to access capital and funding.

One solution is to create more women-led venture capital funds that focus on investing in women-owned businesses. Another is to provide training and resources to help women entrepreneurs improve their financial literacy and access funding from traditional sources.

3. Promote Financial Literacy and Education for Women

Financial literacy and education are essential for women to succeed in the finance ecosystem. Women need to understand how to manage their finances, invest wisely, and navigate the complex financial landscape.

To promote financial literacy and education for women, we need to provide more resources and training programs. This can include workshops, online courses, and mentorship opportunities.

4. Encourage Women to Pursue Careers in Finance

Women are underrepresented in finance careers, particularly in areas such as trading and investment banking. To create a more gender-inclusive finance ecosystem, we need to encourage more women to pursue careers in finance.

This can be done by providing role models and mentorship opportunities for women in finance. Companies can also create policies that promote work-life balance and flexibility, which can help women balance their career and family responsibilities.

In conclusion, creating a more gender-inclusive finance ecosystem is essential for economic growth and social progress. By increasing women's representation in leadership positions, providing access to capital and funding opportunities, promoting financial literacy and education, and encouraging women to pursue careers in finance, we can break down barriers and empower women in the finance industry.

The Future of Women in Finance

The future of women in finance is bright and promising. While the industry has traditionally been male-dominated, women are breaking barriers and making significant strides in this field.

One factor driving this change is the increasing recognition of the importance of diversity and inclusion in the workplace. Companies are realizing that having a diverse workforce leads to better decision-making, increased innovation, and improved financial performance. As a result, more and more firms are actively seeking to attract and retain talented women in finance.

Another factor is the growing number of women who are pursuing careers in finance. Women now make up nearly half of all business school graduates, and many are choosing to specialize in finance. This trend is likely to continue as more women are exposed to the opportunities and rewards that come with a career in finance.

However, there are still challenges that women in finance face. One of the biggest is the persistent gender pay gap. Women in finance earn, on average, 20% less than their male counterparts. This gap is even wider for women of color. Addressing this issue will require companies to be transparent about their pay practices and take concrete steps to ensure that women are paid fairly.

Another challenge is the lack of female representation in leadership positions. While there are many talented women in finance, they are often underrepresented in top management roles. This can make it difficult for women to advance in their careers and can also contribute to a lack of diversity in decision-making.

To address these challenges, it is important for companies to prioritize diversity and inclusion in their hiring and promotion practices. This includes actively seeking out and recruiting talented women, as well as providing training and support to help women advance in their careers.

Overall, the future of women in finance is bright. With increasing recognition of the importance of diversity and inclusion in the workplace, and a growing number of talented women pursuing careers in finance, there is reason to be optimistic about the progress that can be made in this field. However, it will require continued effort and commitment from companies and individuals alike to ensure that women are able to fully realize their potential in finance and other industries.

Empowering Women in the Arts

Challenges Faced by Women in the Arts

The arts have always been a male-dominated industry, and women have faced various challenges in their pursuit of a career in this field. Though women have made significant strides in recent years, there are still many barriers that they have to overcome.

One of the primary challenges faced by women in the arts is the lack of representation. Women are often underrepresented in galleries, museums, and exhibitions, which makes it difficult for them to get recognition for their work. This lack of representation also affects the art market, where women's work is often undervalued compared to male artists.

Another challenge faced by women in the arts is the societal expectation of gender roles. Women are expected to take on traditional roles such as caregiving and nurturing, which can be at odds with the demanding and often unpredictable nature of a career in the arts. This can make it difficult for women to balance their personal life and their career.

Women in the arts also face challenges related to discrimination and harassment. Sexual harassment and gender discrimination are prevalent in the arts industry, and women are often subjected to these behaviors from their colleagues and superiors. This can create a hostile work environment and limit women's opportunities for advancement.

Finally, women in the arts also face challenges related to funding and resources. Women artists often have limited access to funding and resources compared to their male counterparts. This can make it difficult for them to produce and promote their work, limiting their exposure and opportunities for success.

To overcome these challenges, it is essential to promote gender equality and representation in the arts. This can be achieved by supporting women artists, providing equal opportunities for funding and resources, addressing discrimination and harassment, and promoting the work of women artists through exhibitions, galleries, and museums.

In conclusion, women in the arts face numerous challenges, including underrepresentation, gender roles, discrimination, and limited resources. By promoting gender equality and representation, we can create a more diverse and inclusive arts industry that empowers women to pursue their passion and achieve success.

The Importance of Women in the Arts

The arts have been a male-dominated industry for centuries, with women being vastly underrepresented in all forms of artistic expression. However, women have always played a significant role in the arts, and their contributions cannot be ignored. The importance of women in the arts cannot be overstated, and it is time for us to recognize and celebrate their achievements.

Women have been creating art for as long as men have, but their work has often been overlooked or dismissed as inferior. It was not until the feminist movement of the 1960s and 1970s that women artists began to receive recognition and respect for their work. This movement brought attention to the fact that women have been systematically excluded from the art world, and it inspired a new generation of female artists to challenge the status quo.

Today, women continue to make significant contributions to the arts in all its forms. They are painters, sculptors, photographers, writers, musicians, and performers. They are storytellers, and their work reflects their experiences and perspectives as women. They bring a unique voice to the arts, and their contributions have enriched the world of culture and creativity.

The importance of women in the arts goes beyond their artistic achievements. Women in the arts have also been trailblazers in breaking down gender stereotypes and challenging societal norms. They have used their work as a platform to address issues such as gender inequality, sexual harassment, and reproductive rights, among others.

Moreover, women in the arts have been instrumental in empowering other women. They have created spaces for women artists to showcase their work, mentored emerging female artists, and advocated for gender diversity in the arts. By doing so, they have helped to create a more inclusive and equitable environment for women in the arts.

In conclusion, the importance of women in the arts cannot be overstated. Their contributions to the world of culture and creativity have been immense, and their work has challenged societal norms and paved the way for future generations. It is time for us to recognize and celebrate their achievements and to continue to support and empower women in the arts.

Creating a More Gender-Inclusive Arts Ecosystem

The arts industry has been traditionally male-dominated, with women struggling to break through the barriers and achieve recognition for their talents. However, with the rise of the #MeToo movement and increasing awareness of gender inequality, there has been a growing push for a more gender-inclusive arts ecosystem.

One of the key ways to create a more gender-inclusive arts ecosystem is by increasing representation and visibility of women in all aspects of the industry. This includes not just artists, but also directors, producers, curators, and other decision-makers. By ensuring that women have a seat at the table, their perspectives and experiences can be included in the creative process, leading to more diverse and innovative works.

Another important step is to address the gender pay gap in the arts industry. Women are often paid less than men for the same work, and this disparity is particularly pronounced in the arts. By ensuring that women are paid fairly for their work, we can create a more equitable and sustainable arts ecosystem.

It is also important to recognize and address the unique challenges faced by women in the arts industry. For example, women may face discrimination and harassment in the workplace, or struggle to balance their artistic pursuits with caregiving responsibilities. By providing support and resources to women in the arts, we can help them overcome these challenges and thrive in their careers.

Finally, we must continue to celebrate and elevate the work of women artists. By recognizing their contributions to the arts and amplifying their voices, we can inspire future generations of women to pursue their artistic passions.

In conclusion, creating a more gender-inclusive arts ecosystem requires a concerted effort from all stakeholders in the industry. By increasing representation and visibility, addressing the gender pay gap, supporting women artists, and celebrating their work, we can create a more equitable and vibrant arts community.

The Future of Women in the Arts

Women have made significant contributions to the arts throughout history, but their achievements have often been overlooked or undervalued. In recent years, however, there has been a growing recognition of the importance of women's voices and perspectives in the arts, and a movement towards greater gender equality and diversity in the arts world.

The future of women in the arts is bright, but there is still much work to be done to break down barriers and create a more inclusive and supportive environment. Here are some of the key trends and challenges facing women in the arts today:

1. Representation and Visibility

One of the biggest challenges facing women in the arts is a lack of representation and visibility. Women are often underrepresented in galleries, museums, and other art spaces, and their work may be undervalued or overlooked. This can make it difficult for women artists to gain recognition and build a career in the arts.

To address this issue, there are a number of initiatives and organizations working to promote women artists and increase their visibility. For example, the Women's Art Library in London is dedicated to collecting and preserving the work of women artists, while the Women's Caucus for Art is a national organization that advocates for gender equity in the arts.

2. Funding and Resources

Another challenge facing women in the arts is a lack of funding and resources. Women artists may struggle to access the same funding and support as their male counterparts, which can make it difficult to create and exhibit their work.

To address this issue, there are a number of grants, fellowships, and other funding opportunities available specifically for women artists. For example, the Joan Mitchell Foundation provides grants and support to female artists working in painting, sculpture, and other media.

3. Intersectionality and Diversity

Finally, it is important to recognize that women in the arts are not a monolithic group. Women come from diverse backgrounds and experiences, and their perspectives and contributions to the arts are shaped by a range of factors including race, ethnicity, sexual orientation, and disability.

To create a truly inclusive and diverse arts world, it is important to address these intersectional issues and ensure that all women have equal opportunities to succeed in the arts. This may involve creating more opportunities for underrepresented groups, providing support and mentorship to women from diverse backgrounds, and promoting greater awareness and understanding of the intersecting issues facing women in the arts.

In conclusion, the future of women in the arts is bright, but there is still much work to be done to break down barriers and create a more inclusive and supportive environment. By promoting greater representation, providing funding and resources, and addressing intersectional issues, we can create a more equitable and vibrant arts world that truly reflects the diversity and creativity of all women.

Empowering Women in Health and Wellness

Barriers Faced by Women in Health and Wellness

The importance of health and wellness cannot be overemphasized as it is a major determinant of the quality of life. Unfortunately, women face numerous barriers that hinder them from accessing quality health care and achieving optimal wellness.

One of the barriers faced by women in health and wellness is inadequate access to health care services. Women are more likely to experience poverty, which limits their access to health care. Even when they have access to healthcare, they may not receive the quality of care they need due to lack of resources and gender bias.

Another barrier faced by women in health and wellness is gender bias. Gender bias is pervasive in the healthcare system, and it affects the quality of care women receive. For example, women's symptoms are often dismissed as "emotional" or "psychosomatic," and they are less likely to receive appropriate treatment for their conditions.

The lack of representation of women in medical research is another barrier. Women have been historically excluded from medical research, and as a result, many health conditions that affect women are not well understood. This lack of understanding leads to misdiagnosis, inadequate treatment, and poor health outcomes.

In addition, women face cultural and social barriers that hinder their access to health care services. For example, women from certain cultures may not feel comfortable discussing certain health issues with male healthcare providers. Similarly, women from certain communities may not have access to health care due to cultural practices that limit their mobility.

It is important to address these barriers to ensure that women are empowered to take control of their health and wellness. This can be achieved through policy changes that promote gender equity in healthcare, increased representation of women in medical research, and cultural competency training for healthcare providers.

In conclusion, women face numerous barriers in health and wellness, including inadequate access to healthcare, gender bias, lack of representation in medical research, and cultural and social barriers. It is important to address these barriers to promote gender equity in healthcare and empower women to take control of their health and wellness.

The Importance of Women in Health and Wellness

Women play a crucial role in the health and wellness industry. From doctors and nurses to nutritionists and personal trainers, women have been breaking barriers and making significant contributions to the industry. It's essential to recognize the importance of women in health and wellness, not only for the industry but also for society as a whole.

Women are natural caregivers, and their nurturing abilities translate well into the health and wellness industry. Women tend to have an innate ability to empathize with patients and clients, creating a more personalized and compassionate approach to care. This approach has been shown to improve patient outcomes, resulting in better health and wellness for individuals and communities.

Moreover, women are often the primary caregivers in families, making them the gatekeepers of health decisions for their loved ones. Women's understanding of health and wellness can influence the health and wellness choices of their families, leading to better outcomes for all.

Women also bring diversity to the health and wellness industry. In the past, the industry has been dominated by men, leading to a lack of representation and understanding of women's health issues. With women breaking barriers and taking on leadership roles in the industry, there is a more holistic and inclusive approach to health and wellness.

It's essential to empower women in the health and wellness industry to continue breaking barriers and making significant contributions. By providing equal opportunities, support, and recognition, women can continue to innovate and make a difference in the industry.

In conclusion, women are essential to the health and wellness industry. Their natural caregiving abilities, understanding of family health, and diversity bring a unique perspective that can benefit individuals and communities. Empowering women in health and wellness is crucial to continue breaking barriers and making a positive impact in the industry.

Creating a More Gender-Inclusive Health and Wellness Ecosystem

Gender inclusivity is a vital aspect of any workplace, and it is particularly crucial in the health and wellness industry. The industry often perpetuates gender stereotypes, which can lead to women being excluded from certain areas of health and wellness. To create a more gender- inclusive health and wellness ecosystem, it is essential to address these stereotypes and promote an environment that welcomes everyone.

One of the most significant challenges in creating a gender-inclusive health and wellness ecosystem is the lack of representation. Women are underrepresented in leadership positions, and this can lead to a lack of understanding of women's health issues. It is vital to promote more women to leadership positions, which will create a more inclusive environment and a better understanding of women's health needs.

Another challenge is the perpetuation of gender stereotypes in the industry. For example, the fitness industry often promotes the idea that women need to be thin to be healthy. This stereotype is harmful and excludes women of all shapes and sizes. To create a more inclusive environment, it is essential to recognize and challenge these stereotypes.

One way to promote gender inclusivity in the health and wellness industry is to offer services that cater to women's specific needs. For example, offering women-only fitness classes can create a safe and welcoming space for women to exercise. This will help to break down the barriers that prevent women from participating in certain areas of health and wellness.

It is also important to promote education on women's health issues. Many women's health issues are not widely discussed or understood, which can lead to women feeling isolated and excluded from the conversation. By promoting education on women's health issues, we can create a more inclusive environment where women feel comfortable discussing their health concerns.

In conclusion, creating a more gender-inclusive health and wellness ecosystem is essential to promoting equality in the workplace. By promoting women to leadership positions, challenging gender stereotypes, offering services that cater to women's needs, and promoting education on women's health issues, we can create a more inclusive environment where everyone feels welcome and valued.

The Future of Women in Health and Wellness

The world of health and wellness has been predominantly male-dominated for centuries, with women being excluded from decision-making positions and leadership roles. However, with the recent surge of women empowerment movements, this narrative is changing, and the future of women in health and wellness looks brighter than ever before.

Women have always been at the forefront of healthcare, providing care and support to their families and communities. However, even with the critical role women play in healthcare, they have been underrepresented in leadership positions, research, and policy-making. This has led to the exclusion of women's voices in decision-making, leading to a lack of attention to women's health issues.

The future of women in health and wellness is promising as more women are taking up leadership positions, conducting research, and creating policies that address women's health issues. Women are now involved in the development of new drugs, medical devices, and other healthcare technologies that cater to women's specific needs.

The empowerment of women in health and wellness is not limited to the medical field alone. Women are also taking up leadership positions in the fitness and wellness industry, creating products and services that cater to women's unique needs. Women's fitness wear, supplements, and other wellness products are now becoming more inclusive and accessible to all women.

The future of women in health and wellness is also about creating a more supportive and inclusive environment for women. Women's health issues have often been dismissed or minimized, leading to a lack of attention and resources. However, with more women in leadership positions, there is a greater focus on women's health issues, leading to better research and policy-making.

In conclusion, the future of women in health and wellness is promising, and we are witnessing a significant shift in the industry. Women are now taking up leadership positions, conducting research, and creating policies that address women's health issues. As we move forward, it is crucial to continue empowering women and creating a more inclusive and supportive environment for women in health and wellness. This will lead to better healthcare outcomes for all women, and ultimately, a healthier and happier society.

Conclusion

Recap of the Importance of Breaking Barriers and Empowering Women

The fight for gender equality has been ongoing for centuries, and while progress has been made, there is still a long way to go. Women have faced numerous obstacles when it comes to breaking barriers and achieving success in various fields, including the workplace, sports, politics, education, entrepreneurship, leadership, technology, finance, the arts, and health and wellness. The importance of breaking these barriers and empowering women cannot be overstated.

Empowering women means giving them the tools, resources, and opportunities they need to succeed in their chosen field. It means creating an environment that is inclusive and supportive of women, where they can thrive and reach their full potential. Empowering women also means breaking down the cultural and societal barriers that have held them back for so long.

When women are empowered, they can make a significant impact in their respective fields. In the workplace, women can bring a diverse perspective, innovative ideas, and a unique approach to problem-solving. In sports, women can inspire others and show that there is no limit to what they can achieve. In politics, women can bring a fresh perspective to issues and fight for policies that benefit all people, not just a select few. In education, women can inspire and mentor the next generation of leaders. In entrepreneurship, women can create successful businesses that contribute to the economy. In leadership, women can inspire and motivate others to achieve their goals. In technology, women can bring creativity and innovation to the industry. In finance, women can contribute to the growth and success of the industry. In the arts, women can create meaningful and impactful works that inspire others. In health and wellness, women can make a difference in people's lives by promoting healthy lifestyles and providing care and support.

Breaking barriers and empowering women is not just about achieving gender equality; it is about creating a better world for all. When women are given the opportunity to succeed, everyone benefits. It is time to break down the barriers that have held women back for too long and empower them to achieve their full potential. As a society, we must continue to work towards creating a more inclusive and supportive environment for women in all fields. By doing so, we can create a brighter future for everyone.

Final Thoughts and Call to Action

As we come to the end of this book, we hope that you have gained a deeper understanding of the challenges women face in the workplace and the various ways in which you can help empower them. It is important to remember that gender equality is not just a women's issue, but a human issue that affects us all. The success of women in various industries will benefit society as a whole.

We urge both men and women to take action in empowering women in the workplace, sports, politics, education, entrepreneurship, leadership, technology, finance, arts, and health and wellness. Here are some ways you can make a difference:

1. Educate yourself: Learn more about the issues women face in your industry and how to be an ally. Attend workshops or webinars, read books or articles, and engage in conversations with women in your workplace.

2. Be a mentor: If you are in a position of influence, mentor women and provide them with the support and guidance they need to succeed. Encourage them to take on leadership roles and help them develop the skills they need to advance in their careers.

3. Advocate for change: Speak up when you see discrimination or unfair treatment towards women. Push for policies and practices that promote gender equality in the workplace, such as equal pay and flexible working hours.

4. Support women-owned businesses: Invest in women-owned businesses and support their products and services. By doing so, you are helping to close the gender gap in entrepreneurship and promoting economic growth.

5. Self-reflect: Take a moment to reflect on your own biases and how they may be affecting your interactions with women in the workplace. Challenge yourself to be more inclusive and supportive of all your colleagues.

In conclusion, breaking barriers and empowering women in the workplace is a journey that requires collective effort. Let us all work together towards a future where gender equality is a reality, and women are able to achieve their full potential in all aspects of life. Remember, the success of women is not just for women, but for the greater good of society.